Wood Logan Associates, Inc.
&
Venture Annuities
thank you & welcome you
to Lana`i.

Aloha!

2/97

LANA'I
HAWAII

Photography and Text by Arnold Savrann

*This book is dedicated to Gary Onuma who generously
shared the knowledge and wisdom of his lifetime on Lana'i.*

*The author wishes to thank David H. Murdock for
his support and encouragement.*

Copyright © Arnold Savrann/Castle & Cooke, Inc. 1989

Library of Congress Catalog Card Number 89-81452

ISBN 0-9611512-9-3

FOREWORD

by

David H. Murdock

Chairman and Chief Executive Officer
Castle & Cooke, Inc.

When fog bathes the peaks along the Munro Trail, when tall pines become mere silhouettes within the restless clouds, when the mist occasionally parts to permit a glimpse of the sun's reflection on the sea far below — that is when Lana'i becomes frozen in time. At these times, you can hear the earth . . . feel the air . . . smell the wind's bounty, and see history. It is here . . . on Lana'i . . . that you can touch the very soul of man.

Lana'i offers refuge to deer, sheep, quail, partridge, and wild turkey who roam freely here. It boasts of 40 species of plants which grow nowhere else on Earth. Unique soil and climate conditions nurture the best pineapples grown anywhere. Organically grown fruits and vegetables complement the island's natural riches.

To preserve this island's distinctive character, we have carefully constructed two new resorts, new homes, shops, and activity centers for the people who live here and the people we invite to see and experience this exceptional island.

*In the highlands near Lana'i City, the entry to the **Lodge at Ko'ele** is marked by an avenue of pines. Great copper-roofed structures are linked by a grand front porch. Ancient banyan trees, eucalyptus, and jacaranda stand guard, as if to protect the Lodge.*

Dense pine and albizzia forests, vibrant meadows, lush valleys, pineapple fields, and mountain trails surround the Lodge. These natural characteristics define the setting and form of the structures we have designed.

The Lodge at Ko'ele is comfortable within its environment. Its history and legendary tales are an integral part.

Ko'ele is a place of refuge and activity . . . a Kama'aina place . . . uniquely Hawaiian.

A. SAVRANN

*Situated on a slope above the beach at Hulopo'e, the **Manele Bay Hotel** has tiled roofs with overhangs, arcaded loggias, flowered trellises, and lush courtyards brimming with exotic flowers. Gentle waterfalls, well tended lawns, and varieties of palms complete the landscape. Manele's architecture is born of the same Kama'aina traditions that inspired the Lodge at Ko'ele, but here, the warm sun and the sea have contributed to the mediterranean characteristics of the buildings.*

Landscape and architecture complement each other. Manele is a place where one's senses can rediscover the inherent beauty of the natural and the created environment.

Lana'i is a small island, but it has the richness and variety of an entire continent. Our team of architects, landscape architects and interior designers, working closely with me, have endeavored to impart our respect for Hawaii's history, culture and natural environment. These new developments will continue the traditions that are such an integral part of Hawaii.

I invite you to share with me, the Island of Lana'i.

LANA'I

LĀNA'I

Lahaina'Lele

The mystery of Lana'i lies rooted in its history…a history that is both legend and fact. It tells us of a King's son who departed Lahaina'Lele on the island of Maui to challenge the evil spirits who once lived on Lana'i.

His success opened the island to habitation. Its abundant waters, fertile land, and varied climate welcomed these early settlers.

Despite violent battles and decimating diseases during its early history, this sacred isle now prospers…this land called Lana'i.

Island of Lana'i

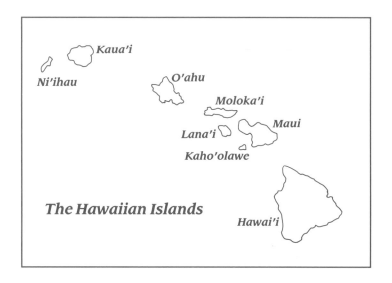

The Hawaiian Islands

Kaua'i
Ni'ihau
O'ahu
Moloka'i
Lana'i
Maui
Kaho'olawe
Hawai'i

Thirteen miles wide and 18 miles long…an arid sea coast…cool green highlands…mountain peaks bathed in mist…

Born of volcanoes, earthquakes, and giant tidal waves …sixth largest among the Hawaiian Islands…myriad microclimates…endless variety of plant types…constantly changing landscape…

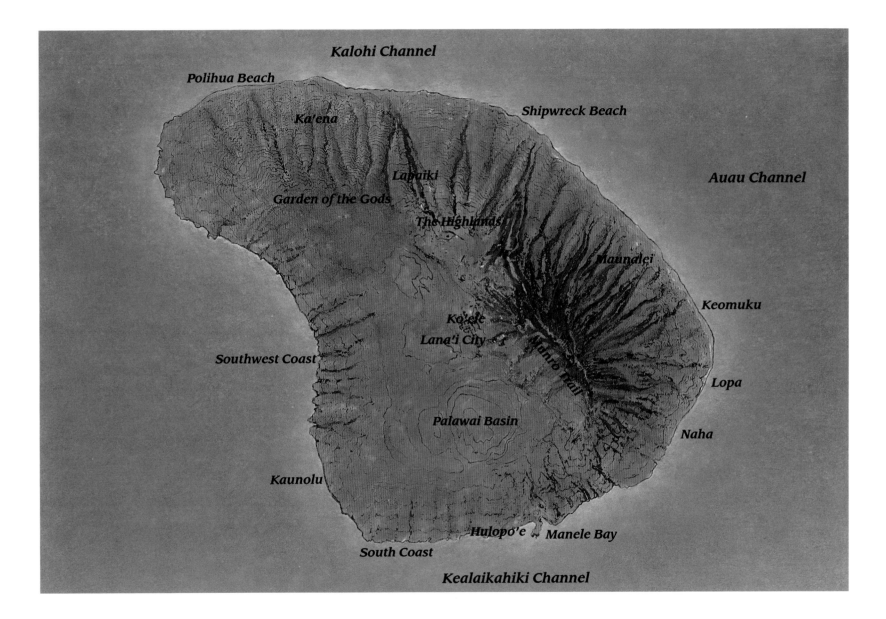

Kalohi Channel

Polihua Beach

Ka'ena

Shipwreck Beach

Auau Channel

Lapaiki

Garden of the Gods

The Highlands

Maunalei

Keomuku

Ko'ele

Lana'i City

Munro Trail

Southwest Coast

Lopa

Palawai Basin

Naha

Kaunolu

Hulopo'e   Manele Bay

South Coast

Kealaikahiki Channel

Manele Bay

Seemingly carved out of the volcanic cliffs and lava rock ledges which surround it, the small boat harbor at Manele has been an historic landing place for many of the island's first visitors.

Pu'u Pehe

Sweetheart rock stands guard over Sharks Bay and the turbulent waters which frequently characterize this place.

According to legend, Pu'u Pehe...a young girl... drowned in a sea cave. Her lover, with help from the gods, carried her body to the summit and buried her beneath the ruins of what is believed to be an ancient bird shrine.

Hulopo'e

A natural bridge provides a gateway to shallow waters and tidepools caught in lava rock crevasses. This is a protected place... a marine life sanctuary.

Hulopo'e Beach

Coconut palms, a crescent of white sand, and a nearby black rock beach share the warm waters of Hulopo'e Bay.

The Palawai Basin

Thousands of years ago, the cone of an extinct volcano collapsed and created this vast plateau encompassing more than 15,000 acres.

The mountains and the sea provide the protective veil that maintains the special climate and soil conditions so well suited for growing pineapples.

Pineapples

Lana'i . . . the Pineapple Island. Nearly one-fifth of Lana'i is devoted to the cultivation of pineapples. Neat rows of spiny bluegreen plants, bright orange fruit, and field workers wrapped in multicolored layers of protective clothing present a kaleidoscope of color.

Banyan, Albizzia, and Kiawe

At Koʻele, giant Banyan roots reach 90 feet to water.

Albizzia survive the elements, in a valley near Lalakoa.

In the hot, dry climate at Manele, a Kiawe tree struggles to maintain its mantle of green.

Kiawe

Albizzia

Banyan

Lana'i City

In 1924, Lana'i City began as a simple plantation town with only 150 residents.

Today, with a much larger population, Lana'i City still retains much of its early character. Small houses with brightly colored rolled-tin roofs line the streets. Interspersed with the vegetable and flower gardens are tall pines, flowering trees, and an array of colorful backyard paraphernalia.

The Dole Shop

A unique expression of convenience and utility. Windows exist in a haphazard pattern, occurring where they best serve interior needs. It is a statement of simple function and classic honesty.

Dole Park

Located in the center of Lana'i City is Dole Park with its more than 100 Cook Island pines each reaching over 90 feet in height.

Shops, offices, recreational buildings, and churches line the edges of the park. Together with the venerable Hotel Lana'i, this area is the social center of Lana'i City.

The Pines at Ko'ele

First introduced in the late 19th century, the Norfolk Island and Cook Island pines have become characteristic symbols of Lana'i.

Anthurium, Hibiscus, and O'hia

Wildflowers and bromeliads are among the more than 40 native plant species that grow in the upland plateaus, arid lowlands, mountain valleys, and rainforests.

O'hia

Day Lily

Poinsettia

Bird of Paradise

Red Ginger

Anthurium

Hibiscus

The Highlands of Mahana

Mouflon sheep and axis deer inhabit this cool, moist environment where forests, gentle valleys, and tall grasses offer food and protection.

Pinnacles at Wawaeku

An eerie landscape of giant pinnacles resulted from centuries of wind-driven water and sand. Soil erosion exposed these limestone spires and created a place that continues to be shaped by the elements.

The Polihua Road

Boulders are supported by fragile eddies of earth. Giant sisal and an ironwood forest challenge the erosive forces of nature.

Lapaiki

*In canyons carved by wind and water, the high iron
content of the earth has oxidized and become a sculptor's
garden and a painter's palette of exuberant color.*

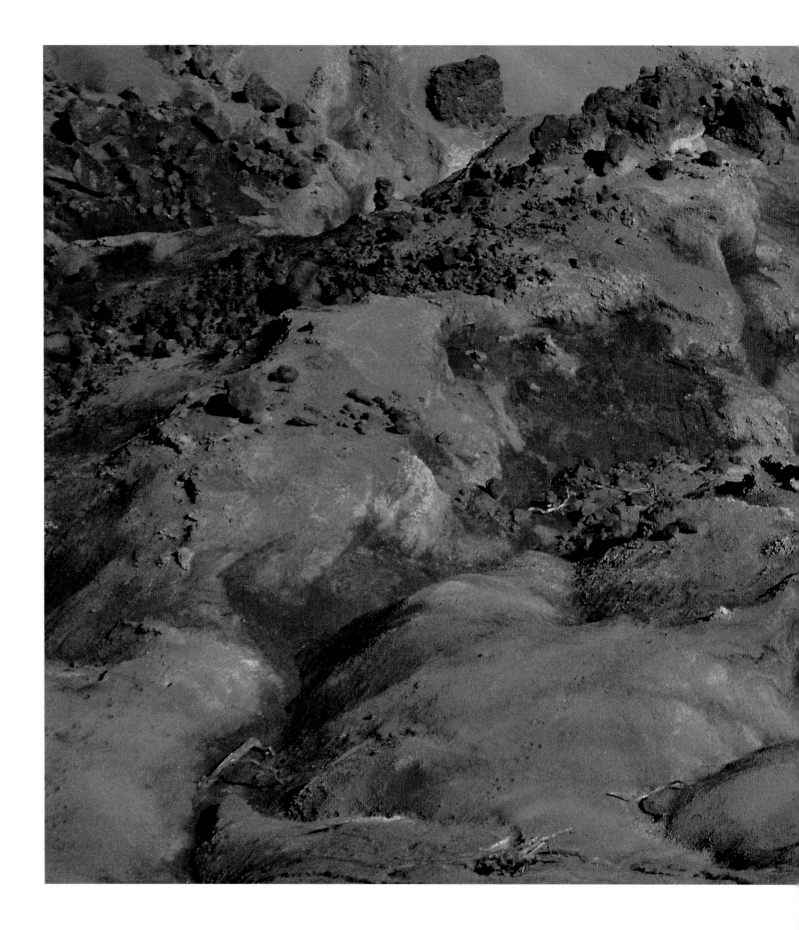

Garden of the Gods

Centuries of relentless winds have eroded this once luxuriant landscape. Multicolored rocks and giant boulders, perhaps placed here by a great volcanic tidal wave, dominate this desolate area with the ancient name Ka'a...the barren land.

Although nature originally shaped this place, man has, with equal deliberation, carefully constructed the stone cairns which stand silently, defiantly as tributes to loved ones.

Ka'ena

Beyond the Garden of the Gods the Ka'ena Road descends toward the island's most westerly point . . . Land's End.

The rock strewn landscape of the higher elevations gives way to expanses of luminescent Pili grass and canyons sculpted of red earth.

Huawai Bay and the South Coast

Green plateaus meet the sea, interrupted by sheer walls of stone, and rocky promontories.

The warm waters welcome humpback whales during winter months.

Kaunolu

*A great Kiawe tree grows, alone on a
plateau high above the sea. This sacred site
is mute testimony to a time when volcanoes
and tidal waves created this land.*

*Legends and stories of evil spirits
were born from within the secret caves
which etch the cliffs at the water's edge.*

*For many thousands of years thereafter,
this strange and beautiful place remained in
isolation, even from its neighbor islands.*

*The Kiawe tree at Kaunolu is a
sentinel over a lonely and mysterious past.*

Heiaus, Caves, and Petroglyphs

The district...ahupuaa...of Kaunolu was a place of refuge...a holy place where King Kamehameha and his priests built homes and temples, and spent summers fishing in the "Royal Waters."

At Kaunolu, history is seen in the ruins, heard in the caves, and told in stone etchings.

Ilima and Kahekili

A field of delicate Ilima, a favorite sweet smelling lei flower, contrasts with the legendary Kahekili's Drop...where one's life depended on a skillful plunge to the sea below.

The Southwest Coast . . . Kaunolu to Nanahoa

The cliffs of Kaholo Pali, rock beaches, caves, and giant pinnacles create a shoreline of changing sounds and dramatic visual images.

Polihua Beach and the North Shore

Windswept and remote, this is the largest white sand beach on Lana'i. Poli…cove, hua…eggs, is the legendary nesting place of the Hawaiian Green Sea Turtle, once favored by the Goddess Pele because of her fondness for their eggs.

The shallow waters of the Kalohi channel are a favorite place for island fishermen.

Shipwreck Beach

Awalua, Lapaiki, Kahue, and Pō'aīwa are some of the names which comprise the eight miles of shore from Polihua to Kahokunui. Black sands, rock ledges, fresh water seeps, dunes, and kukio grasses give each part of this coast a special character.

Along the northern shore, unpredictable winds, ocean currents, and sometimes the deliberate will of man have placed many ships onto the shallow off-shore reefs. This varied stretch of coastline has come to be known as Shipwreck Beach.

Maunalei

The "Mountain of Lei" derives its name from the small flower-like clouds which oftentimes surround the highest peaks bordering this remote valley.

Maunalei was a favorite place of Gods and chieftains because of its tropical plants and abundant wildlife.

Keomuku

The Kalanakila o ka Malamalama Church and the coconut grove which surrounds it are reminders of the once thriving community which existed here.

Lopa

South of Keomuku, secluded and pristine white sand beaches line the coast to Naha.

Naha

At the end of the Keomuku Road, there is an ancient fish pond. Legends abound in this place, and it is here that much of the early history of Lana'i began.

From this eastern shore warriors built a foot path to the Palawai Basin.

Legend and history live side by side...at Naha...

Munro Trail

For more than seven miles, a narrow road winds its way among mountain peaks and gorges.

Neat rows of pine trees, planted by New Zealand naturalist George Munro, survive the wind and rain which frequent these heights.

Rainforests, Wild Orchids, and Ferns

Almost always bathed in cool mist, the pines, ferns, and dense undergrowth collect moisture and continue to be the source of springs, just as they have been for centuries.

Lana'i-Hale

At Ho'okio Gulch pine trees stand, like soldiers, in tribute to the Lana'ians who once, long ago, defended themselves against militant forces.

Today, from the heights of nearby Lanai-Hale, only a peacefulness is felt.

Far below, Lana'i presents a silent, quilted landscape.

Lana'i is a timeless island in a sea of change.
It is a study of harmony in contrast.

Lana'i is a place of hot sun and cool mist.
It is a home for desert flowers and rain forests.

Lana'i is a place of sheer cliffs and sparkling beaches.
It is a tidepool and a waterspout amidst rocky outcroppings.

Lana'i is a wild orchid, a field of pineapples, and stately pines.
It is a place where things grow and the spirit soars.

Lana'i is a place of rare beauty and enduring natural riches.
It is history captured and time forgotten.